Attitude:

Your Key to Success

FOUNDED 1870

About the Authors

Michele Matt Yanna is the founder and president of The TRAINERS Group, Inc., an international training company. As a professional trainer, facilitator, consultant, project manager, and national presenter, she has worked with the attitudes of employees and managers from a variety of industries.

Adapted for the American Correctional Association by Ida M. Halasz, Ph.D. Ida Halasz served as the Deputy Administrator of the National Institute of Corrections Academy, U.S. Department of Justice. The Academy is a federal agency dedicated to providing training, technical assistance, and information to state, local, and federal correctional agencies.

Foreword

It has been said that "attitude is everything," and in training, nothing is closer to the truth. In my 25 years in the field, I have watched our profession grow by leaps and bounds. The American Correctional Association has been a stalwart advocate for professionalism, job knowledge and consistency in our field. As a diverse group with similar goals, we have established training academies, pre-service and in-service curricula and a host of professional seminars and conferences. In their pursuit of career advancement, correctional employees are offered the best that we have to offer.

In this publication, Dr. Ida M. Halasz and Michele Matt Yanna have combined their considerable experience and talent in the field of training and given us a "how to" manual on shaping attitudes. *Attitude: Your Key to Success* is a practical tool that can be used to understand where our attitudes come from, how they influence almost every aspect of our daily lives, and how we can—if motivated—change those negative attitudes into positive ones.

The authors advise the reader to keep the workbook close at hand and use it as a "coach to support your goals, encourage your successes, and rechannel your attitudes." As corrections leaders and managers, we know that a positive attitude yields a positive result. We can all use this resource first to help us understand our own motivations. Subsequently, we can use the tools we've acquired to assist staff who display negative attitudes and help them rechannel their outlook. At the same time, the publication can assist us in identifying and supporting people who serve as positive forces in our organizations.

As president of the American Correctional Association, I am proud to support the efforts and creativity of those who work to shape correctional leaders. I urge you to make good use of this "Key to Success," both in your personal and professional lives.

Reginald A. Wilkinson
President, American Correctional Association
and
Director
Ohio Department of Rehabilitation and Correction

a publication of the
AMERICAN CORRECTIONAL ASSOCIATION
4380 Forbes Boulevard
Lanham, Maryland 20706-4322
(301) 918-1800
Fax: (301) 918-1900
http://www.corrections.com/ACA

How to Use This Book

The primary goal of this workbook is to help you gain control of your attitude in order to better deal with living and working in a complex world. Working in corrections is especially difficult. It requires constant awareness of safety and security. It requires an acceptance that offenders often have deceptive and harmful attitudes. This makes it even more difficult to work with them on an ongoing basis and to maintain your own positive attitude. This workbook will help you understand how influential your attitude is in gaining control over your personal and work lives. You'll find that it contains practical yet powerful techniques to help you appreciate, analyze, adjust, and maintain a positive attitude. This workbook will help you if you:

- Want to gain more control of your life at home or at work.

- Have difficulty accepting change.

- Want to improve your relationships with other people, such as offenders, co-workers, family members, and those you supervise.

- Avoid taking risks or accepting challenges.

- Want to enjoy a more fulfilling and happier life.

Use This Workbook Often

Keep this workbook close at hand as a ready resource. Think of it as a coach to support your goals, encourage your successes, and rechannel your attitudes. Use the Table of Contents as a quick reference guide.

To fully experience the potential of this workbook, use a highlighter to mark statements, quotations, or ideas that you find valuable. Answer the questions in the interactive exercises, and jot down notes in the outer margins as you read the chapters. Use the workbook as a tool to capture your important thoughts and ideas about your attitudes.

The authors and The American Correctional Association hope that this workbook truly helps you gain control of your attitude and improve your life.

Table of Contents

Chapter One

HOW TO UNDERSTAND YOUR ATTITUDE

Chapter Objectives

After completing this chapter, you should be able to:

- Describe why attitudes are so important in life.

- Explain where attitudes come from and how they are formed.

- Define the parts of an attitude. Describe and recognize three types of attitudes: Positive, Negative, and Neutral.

- Use a formula to calculate your attitude and anticipated action.

Our Lifetime Companions

They've been with you since you were born, and they're with you wherever you go—at work, at home, at school, and even on the streets. Some days, you're glad to have them around, but on other days, you may wish that they had stayed in bed! We all have them—some are good, and some aren't. In fact, you've been around them so much, you're probably good at detecting them in others. We're talking about our lifetime companions—our attitudes!

> . . . you're probably good at detecting them in others.

A Good Attitude Leads to Success

Telemetrics International recently surveyed 16,000 people to identify the common traits of successful people—or high achievers. The high achievers tended to:

- Care about people, as well as the bottom line.

- Respect the value of other people's abilities.

- Seek advice from others.

- Be good listeners.

- Have a positive attitude about life in general.

You Control Your Attitude

There are so many things in life you have little or no control over, such as the weather, the job market, and the economy. But there's one aspect of your life that you do have the power to control, and that's your attitude. Each and every moment of every day, you decide what your attitude will be—about yourself, your job, your family and friends, the offenders you work with , change, responsibility, and so on.

Certainly, other factors influence your attitude, such as your past experiences and the experiences of those around you. But no one can make you feel anything without your permission. You hold the remote control to the channels of energy that create both your attitude and your results in life.

So, to gain control of your life, you must learn to gain control over your attitude. Having a positive attitude can bring about positive results at home and at work that will bring you happiness and success.

. . . no one can make you feel anything without your permission.

What Is an Attitude?

An attitude is a mental stance toward a person, place or thing. It is based on your expectations and perceptions (our definition of reality). To better understand your attitudes, let's examine the major parts that make up an attitude.

Expectations

In any given situation, you have consciously or unconsciously formulated a set of expectations, or desired results, for yourself, for other people, and for situations. Sometimes referred to as your standards, these expectations determine your level of satisfaction. The higher your expectations, the more challenging it will be to feel satisfied with any given situation.

Perception

Your five senses and past experiences create your perception, or interpretation, of a current situation. Based on what you see, hear, smell, touch, and taste, you develop your definition of what happened. Your perception may or may not be an accurate account of what actually happened; however, perception is what you use to formulate your thoughts and feelings about the situation.

Thoughts

Your thoughts define your state of mind. Happy people are most likely thinking happy thoughts. Conversely, sad or angry people are probably having negative thoughts.

Thoughts spark the formation of an attitude. Once your mind is stimulated, you consciously or unconsciously think about the situation.

While they're in progress, thoughts sound like, "I think . . ." or "I believe." Thoughts—like feelings and attitudes—may be expressed out loud or silently to yourself.

Feelings

Your feelings keep your thoughts alive. It's virtually impossible to have an attitude without thoughts or feelings. Feelings encourage more thoughts and keep the mind active. While they're in progress, feelings sound like, "I feel . . ."

Energy

The amount of energy you exert in a relationship or a situation depends on how important the issue is to you. The greater the importance, the more energy you'll use to express your attitude through words, tone of voice, body language, and other behaviors. Like attitudes themselves, this energy can be positive, negative, or neutral in nature.

The greater the importance, the more energy you'll use to express your attitude . . .

Action

An action is your physical response to a situation. Once again, you have the choice of taking a positive, negative, or neutral approach to each situation. Your action will be a reflection of your attitude. A positive action in progress sounds like, "I can . . . " or "I will . . . " In contrast, a negative action in progress sounds like, "I can't . . . " or "I won't . . . " A neutral action in progress sounds like, "I don't want to . . . " or "I don't care . . ."

Attitude Application

The following situation illustrates how an attitude is created and expressed.

The warden and his wife are celebrating their 15th wedding anniversary at their favorite restaurant. After taking the first bite of his meal, the warden is very disappointed. He calls the waiter to their table, pushes his plate of food aside, and states in a firm and deliberate tone, "This food is cold and looks like it's been sitting out all day. I refuse to touch it!"

Based on past experiences from eating at his favorite restaurant, the warden had high **expectations** that the food would look appealing and taste good. However, after tasting this particular meal, his **perception** of the food was just the opposite. He **thought** the food tasted cold and looked stale. He **felt** that the quality of the meal was important to the celebration of the occasion. So, he exerted **energy** by requesting that the waiter come to their table (**action**). He expressed his **attitude** by:

1. Pushing aside his plate of food.

2. Talking in a firm and deliberate tone of voice.

3. Complaining about the food.

Check Your Attitude

Describe a recent situation at your facility or agency, at home, or in public that led you or someone else to illustrate an attitude. Complete the following statements to determine what kind of attitude was expressed.

1. Describe the situation by identifying who was involved and when and where it happened. Who: _____
When: _____
Where: _____

2. Define your **expectations** of what should have happened.

_____
_____
_____

3. Describe your **perception** of what you believe happened.

_____
_____
_____

4. Identify your **thoughts** about the situation by completing the sentence: "I think . . ." or "I believe . . ." _____

_____
_____

5. Identify your **feelings** about the situation by completing the sentence, "I feel . . ." _____

_____
_____

6. Describe your **actions** (both words and behaviors). _____

_____
_____

7. Circle the attitude that best describes your overall reaction to the situation.

Positive   Negative   Neutral

Where Do Attitudes Come From?

Experts generally agree that we develop our attitudes early in life—from birth to age seven. The good news is that we all start out with good attitudes; the bad news is that we later learn how to sour our attitudes.

Consider a baby—full of happiness, curiosity, and acceptance. Babies very seldom reject people based on age, race, sex, color, or ethnic background. They're like sponges, hungry to learn, grow, and experience the many facets of life. Unconsciously, babies recognize that they need other people in order to survive.

So, what happens? We become influenced by our environment. Significant people around us—our parents, guardians, family members, teachers, and friends—pass on their attitudes through their words and actions. Studies show that by the time we are two years old, we observe more than 8,000 hours of life—the good, the bad, and the ugly—plus whatever is on TV.

> . . . we develop our attitudes early in life—from birth to age seven.

The Past Is History

Even though the attitudes we learned at an early age are the most difficult ones to change, they aren't etched in stone. We can unlearn them and relearn new ones. We must recognize that attitudes which worked yesterday may not work today. Remember, you can control your attitudes!

> We can unlearn them and relearn new ones.

Three Types of People, Three Types of Attitudes

There are as many types of attitudes as there are people in our world. However, for our purposes, we'll simplify things a bit and focus on three broad categories of people and their attitudes.

Spectators

Some people go through life watching it happen around them. They're called the spectators of life. Their life experiences are limited because they "play it safe" and avoid risk. They would much rather observe or support others than risk failure or make a mistake. Spectators usually have a neutral attitude about life.

Critics

Another group of people stays on the sidelines of life. We call them the critics. They perceive themselves as experts in the game of life and pride themselves on finding fault in others. They want their complaints to be heard and understood. They often associate with fellow "critics" because they feel comfortable in numbers. Critics usually have a negative attitude about life.

Players take risks and are not afraid to make mistakes.

Players

The third type of people are the players in the game of life. They eagerly await opportunities to learn something new and to grow, both personally and professionally. They take risks and are not afraid to make mistakes. Players usually have a positive attitude about life.

People and their attitudes can change, depending on the situation. Just as no one is completely positive or negative all the time, our attitudes can last only temporarily. For instance, a positive person is capable of demonstrating a negative attitude toward a person or situation. Likewise, a negative person can demonstrate a positive attitude from time to time.

A Typical Situation

You're likely to find all three types of people on every "team," whether it's at your facility or agency, at home, or in the community. Let's say you've just been asked to plan your agency's open house. The "spectators" on the team will attend every meeting. But they won't take an active part in the discussion or volunteer to accept any responsibility. They may even attend the meetings to get out of work.

"Critics" will spend most of their time complaining about last year's open house and criticizing the plans for this year's event. In addition, they'll probably be the first to shoot down other people's ideas for improving it. And finally, the "players" will actively particpate in planning and implementing the open house. They'll follow through to make sure that good ideas are used and tasks are completed. In other words, the players will "take the ball and run with it!"

. . . the players will "take the ball and run with it!"

Check Your Attitude

How would you describe your actions lately at home with your family? At work with co-workers and offenders? In your life in general? What kind of person have you been? How might the people around you describe your attitude? Place a check mark under the personality type that best describes your attitude in the following environments.

	Spectator	Critic	Player
At Home			
At Work			
Co-workers			
Offenders			
In Life			

Are you pleased with the results you've been getting at home, at work, and in your personal life? You may need to make some adjustments to become a better "player" at home, at work, or in life.

The Dynamics of an Attitude

To gain a better understanding of the three types of people, let's take a closer look at how their attitudes are created and expressed. Let's begin by exploring the thoughts and feelings people experience with each type of attitude.

The "Players" with Positive Attitudes

The following list describes some of the **thoughts** of a "player" with a positive attitude.

- There is something good in every situation.

- A problem is an opportunity to do something different.

- Change is a sign of growth.

- A mistake is a valuable step toward success.

- I have control over my life.

The following list describes some of the **feelings** of a "player" with a positive attitude.

- Happy

- Confident

- Satisfied

- Optimistic

- Loving

The "Critics" with Negative Attitudes

The following list describes some of the thoughts of a "critic" with a negative attitude.

- There is always something wrong.

- Other people cause problems.

- Change is a thorn in my side.

- A mistake is a failure.

- I have little or no control over my life.

The following list describes some of the **feelings** of a "critic" with a negative attitude.

- Anger

- Doubt

- Frustration

- Pessimism

- Hate

The "Spectators" with Neutral Attitudes

The following list describes some of the **thoughts** of a "spectator" with a neutral attitude.

- The situation or the other person is unimportant.

- Someone else will solve the problem.

- Change is unnecessary.

- The future will come and go with or without me.

- I won't even try to control my life.

The following list describes some of the **feelings** of a "spectator" with a neutral attitude.

- Unemotional

- Tired

- Content

- Indifferent

- Detached

... we communicate our true meanings more with our tone of voice and body language than with the words we use.

How Are Attitudes Expressed?

You express your attitude in three different ways:

1. The words you use (*what* you say or what you don't say).

2. The tone of voice you use (*how* you say what you say).

3. Body language, such as facial expressions (what you *do*).

Research tells us that we communicate our true meanings more with our tone of voice and body language than with the words we use. Only 8 percent of what we communicate comes from our words. The remaining 92 percent comes from our tone of voice and body language. Let's explore what attitudes sound and look like.

What Do Attitudes Sound Like?

A positive attitude is verbally expressed with action words in an upbeat, enthusiastic tone of voice. Conversely, a negative attitude is verbally expressed with words of resistance in a whining or abrasive tone of voice. A neutral attitude is often expressed through silence; however, it may be expressed with apathy by using passive language in a nonemotional tone of voice.

Listed below are some of the most common words conveyed by each attitude. Read the list to yourself or out loud using a tone of voice appropriate for that attitude.

Positive Language *. . . upbeat voice.*	*Negative Language* *. . . whining or* *abrasive voice.*	*Neutral Language* *. . . nonemotional.*
I can.	I can't.	I don't want to.
I will.	I won't.	I might.
I expect it.	No way.	I doubt it.
I will make time.	I don't have time.	I'll see if I have time.
Positively.	Not.	Maybe.
I'm sure.	I'm afraid.	I don't know.
I choose to.	You made me.	I didn't.
Go.	Stop.	Coast.

Notice how many "n't" words—can't, won't, don't—are associated with negative and neutral attitudes. Learn to eliminate such words from your vocabulary. Learn to think and speak positively. Talk about what you *can* do for yourself and others, not about what you *can't* do. Remember, you can unlearn old attitudes and relearn new ones. You can change them because you control them.

What Do Attitudes Look Like?

Your body language often expresses your attitude more clearly than your words and tone of voice. For example, a smile expresses happiness and a positive attitude. Conversely, a frown expresses anger or frustration and a negative attitude. Hands, arms, and gestures also express your feelings and attitudes. For instance, waving your arms frantically in the air expresses excitement and a positive attitude, while shaking a clenched fist expresses hostility and a negative attitude.

Take a moment . . .

You've heard and seen them all before—positive attitudes, negative attitudes, and neutral attitudes. Take a moment to describe what attitudes look and sound like coming from the three types of people we defined earlier. What does each type do? What do they say? How do they say it? Describe their tone of voice, facial expressions, and other body language.

"Players" with a **positive attitude** are more likely to take the following action. Example: Smile, laugh, and act enthusiastic.

_____

_____

_____

"Critics" with a **negative attitude** are more likely to take the following action. Example: Frown and look disgusted.

_____

_____

_____

"Spectators" with a **neutral attitude** are more likely to take the following action or inaction. Example: Daydream and look expressionless.

_____

_____

_____

How do each of these attitudes usually make you feel?
Positive. Example: Happy. _____
Negative. Example: Upset. _____
Neutral. Example: Frustrated. _____

What Can You Expect from Your Attitude?

As you learned earlier, your thoughts and feelings create your attitude. And your attitude determines your actions, which leads to the results you get in life. Here are several examples of what the three types of attitudes may lead to in your life.

> ... your attitude determines your actions ...

Benefits of a Positive Attitude

Although it's not a guarantee, a positive attitude can help you:

- Get a better job or a promotion.

- Successfully complete a project.

- Achieve a personal or professional goal.

- Work better with offenders.

- Maintain a relationship with a friend, co-worker, or spouse.

Consequences of a Negative Attitude

It would be interesting to know how many times a negative attitude caused someone to:

- Be passed over for a promotion.

- Lose his or her job.

- Fail to achieve a personal or professional goal.

- Lose the opportunity to positively influence an offender.

- Ruin a relationship with a friend, co-worker, or family member.

Consequences of a Neutral Attitude

The apathy expressed by someone with a neutral attitude may cause the person to:

- Miss out on an opportunity.
- Fail to learn new skills or gain needed knowledge.
- Become stagnant in a job or career.
- Fail to develop new relationships.
- Be excluded from an activity.

Attitude Calculation

To gain control of your life, you must first learn to gain control over your thoughts, feelings, and attitudes. To anticipate the kind of action and results you're likely to experience in any given situation, you can use the Attitude Calculation Formula described below:

To gain control of your life, you must first learn to gain control over your thoughts, feelings, and attitudes.

$$\frac{(\text{Thoughts} + \text{Feelings}) \times \text{Attitude}}{\text{Action}}$$

Step 1. Thoughts and Feelings

Begin by assigning a numerical value to your thoughts and your feelings about someone or some situation. Use a 10-point scale, with 1 being extremely poor and 10 being extremely good. Add these values together to arrive at a score for your "perception." With a maximum score of 20, the higher your score, the more favorable your perception of the situation.

Step 2. Attitude

The next step is to assign a value to your

attitude about the situation, using a scale of -10 to +10. To indicate a negative attitude, select a number between -10 and -1, with -10 being extremely negative. To indicate a neutral or passive attitude about the situation, use zero. To indicate a positive attitude, assign a value between +1 and +10, with +10 being extremely positive.

Step 3. Action

The final step is to multiply the value of your perception (the sum of your thoughts and feelings) times the value you assigned to your attitude (-10 to +10) to calculate your anticipated action. You'll discover from this calculation that a positive attitude will create positive action. Conversely, a negative attitude will bring about negative action. A neutral attitude, indicated by a value of zero, will result in little or no action.

Check Your Attitude

Let's try the attitude calculation formula. Think of a situation you need to deal with in the next few days, and calculate your potential results.

Situation (who and what):

1. Assign a value to your thoughts (1 to 10, with 1 extremely poor and 10 extremely good). _____

2. Assign a value to your feelings (1 to 10). _____

3. Add the value you assigned to your thoughts and your feelings. Line 1 Thoughts _____ + Line 2 Feelings _____ = Perception _____ Your combined thoughts and feelings are your perception of the situation.

4. Assign a value to your attitude (-10 to +10, with -10 extremely negative and +10 extremely positive)

5. Multiply the value of your perception (total of Line 3) x the value of your attitude (Line 4).
   _____ Perception
   x _____ Attitude
   _____
   _____ Anticipated Action Value

   Perception x Attitude = Anticipated Action

Evaluating Your Anticipated Action

The higher your score, the greater the results and the higher the satisfaction you will likely enjoy. To raise your score, reconsider your thoughts, feelings and, especially, your attitude about the situation.

> **This attitude calculation illustrates how you become what you think.**

This attitude calculation illustrates how you become what you think. You hold the remote control. You have the power to choose your thoughts and feelings and, therefore, control your attitudes. If you think and feel positively, you will have positive attitudes and enjoy positive results. In the next few chapters, you will learn techniques for analyzing, adusting, and maintaining your attitude.

Chapter Summary

In this chapter, you learned how to recognize the three types of attitudes: positive, negative, and neutral. You discovered that your thoughts and feelings create your attitudes. In turn, your attitudes lead to your actions and the results you get in life.

In the next chapter, you'll tune in to your attitudes and discover what you think and feel about the areas of your life.

Chapter Two

HOW TO ANALYZE YOUR ATTITUDE

Chapter Objectives

After completing this chapter, you should be able to:

- Use the Self-Image Inventory to assess your attitude.

- Recognize the energy you exert at work, at home, and in your personal life because of your attitude.

Your Attitude About You

The first step in gaining control of your attitude is understanding yourself. Take a look in the mirror. What do you see? Your self-image can be your best friend or your worst enemy, depending on its strength or weakness. Your self-image or self-esteem is how you think and feel about yourself as a person. This attitude about yourself determines how you act, how you learn, how you work, how you play, and how you relate to others. How much self-esteem you have also determines how you cope with problems and fulfill your needs. It measures the degree to which you accept, value, respect, regard, rely on, trust, and confide in yourself. If you have a high self-esteem, you have a sense of confidence and reliance in your ability to meet the challenges of life.

> **Your self-image can be your best friend or your worst enemy . . .**

You may compare yourself with other people and become discouraged because you think that others are smarter, better looking,

Recognize, appreciate, and, most importantly, believe in your own abilities, and you'll become more confident and capable.

more talented, or richer than you. This type of comparison isn't healthy and can make you feel discouraged and dissatisfied with yourself. You always will find someone else who is better than you in one area or another. Recognize, appreciate, and, most importantly, believe in your *own* abilities, and you'll become more confident and capable.

Your Self-Image (SI) Inventory *

The Self-Image (SI) Inventory is a questionnaire that you can use to analyze different aspects of your self-image or self-esteem. The SI Inventory is designed to help you describe how you think and feel about yourself. It is an indication of your self-esteem, your self-perception as it relates to others, and your satisfaction with your role in life. It's important to remember, however, that self-image or self-esteem is abstract—it lacks specific boundaries or limits and can't be measured on an absolute scale. Think of the following SI Inventory as a general indicator of your self-image, not an absolute assessment of it.

Directions:

There are no right or wrong answers. The best answer is your honest answer. Avoid answering the questions the way you think others would. Also avoid comparing yourself with other people. Instead, listen to yourself when you determine each response.

* Reprinted with permission from *Becoming the Me I Want to Be,* Simmermacher, Don. R & E Publishsers, Saratoga, California, 1993.

Circle the letter of the response that you feel best fits you.

1. In terms of attractiveness, I am:
   a. Very attractive
   b. Fairly attractive
   c. Average
   d. Fairly unattractive
   e. Very unattractive

2. My personality is:
   a. Very interesting
   b. Fairly interesting
   c. Average
   d. Fairly boring
   e. Very boring

3. I have:
   a. A lot of confidence in myself
   b. Enough confidence in myself
   c. Average confidence in myself
   d. Very little confidence in myself
   e. No confidence in myself

4. I think that I get along with others:
   a. Extremely well
   b. Well
   c. Okay
   d. Not very well
   e. Not well at all

5. When competing with others, I feel:
   a. I will usually win
   b. I have a good chance to win
   c. I will win sometimes
   d. I will usually not win
   e. I never will win

6. I dress:
   a. Very well
   b. Fairly well
   c. Acceptably
   d. Not very well
   e. Sloppily

7. When I walk into a room, I make:
   a. A good impression
   b. A fair impression
   c. An average impression
   d. No impression
   e. A bad impression

8. I accept personal compliments with:
   a. No embarrassment
   b. Little embarrassment
   c. Occasional embarrassment
   d. Frequent embarrassment
   e. Constant embarrassment

9. I feel confident that I will succeed in the future:
   a. All the time
   b. Most of the time
   c. Some of the time
   d. Hardly ever
   e. Never

10. In terms of maturity, I am:
    a. Very mature
    b. Fairly mature
    c. Average
    d. Below average
    e. Immature

11. When among strangers, I feel:
    a. Very comfortable
    b. Fairly comfortable
    c. The same as usual
    d. Uncomfortable
    e. Extremely uncomfortable

12. I feel warm and happy toward (good about) myself:
    a. All the time
    b. Most of the time
    c. Some of the time
    d. Hardly ever
    e. Never

13. If I could make myself all over again, I would be:
    a. Exactly as I am
    b. About the same
    c. Slightly changed
    d. Greatly changed
    e. Another person

14. I experience enjoyment and zest for living:
    a. All the time
    b. Most of the time
    c. Some of the time
    d. Hardly ever
    e. Never

15. I admit my mistakes, shortcomings, and defeats:
    a. All the time
    b. Most of the time
    c. Occasionally
    d. Hardly ever
    e. Never

16. I feel inferior to others:
    a. Never
    b. Hardly ever
    c. Occasionally
    d. Most of the time
    e. All the time

17. I feel that I am in control of my life:
    a. All the time
    b. Most of the time
    c. Some of the time
    d. Seldom
    e. Never

18. I have an intense need for recognition and approval:
    a. None of the time
    b. Hardly ever
    c. Occasionally
    d. Most of the time
    e. All the time

19. I try to live by my own values, beliefs, and convictions:
    a. All the time
    b. Most of the time
    c. Some of the time
    d. Seldom
    e. Never

20. I am able to solve my problems:
    a. All the time
    b. Most of the time
    c. Some of the time
    d. Seldom
    e. Never

21. I avoid new goals or efforts because of fear of mistakes or failures:
    a. Never
    b. Seldom
    c. Some of the time
    d. Most of the time
    e. All the time

22. I believe I am achieving my potential:
    a. All the time
    b. Most of the time
    c. Some of the time
    d. Seldom
    e. Never

23. I believe that rules or guidelines are:
    a. To be respected and followed
    b. To be used if necessary
    c. For others to follow
    d. To be challenged or changed
    e. To be broken

24. When people ask me to do something for them, I feel:
    a. Good, because they trust me to help them; I appreciate the opportunity.
    b. Okay; I'll do it.
    c. Disinterested in helping them; I won't respond immediately.
    d. Bothered by their request; I'll resist accepting the responsibility.
    e. Angry; I won't do it.

Scoring

1. Record the number of responses for each letter (number of a's, b's, c's, d's, and e's)

2. Multiply the number of each letter by its corresponding value.

3. Add each score to get a total score.

SAMPLE					
	a (+2)	b (+1)	c (0)	d (-1)	e (-2)
1. Number	10	5	8	0	2
(times value)	(+2)	(+1)	(0)	(-1)	(-2)
2. Score	20	5	0	0	-4
3. Total Score = scores added (20+5+0+0-4) = 21					

	1.	x	**2.**		
a's:	10	x	2	=	20
b's:	5	x	1	=	5
c's:	8	x	0	=	0
d's:	0	x	-1	=	0
e's:	2	x	-2	=	-4

3. 21 Total Score

	a	**b**	**c**	**d**	**e**
1. Number					
X	**+ 2**	**+ 1**	**0**	**- 1**	**- 2**
2. Score					

3. _____
Total Score

Interpretation

A total score of:	Indicates you have:
-48 to -36	A complete feeling of rejection and inadequacy.
-35 to -17	A significant feeling of rejection and inadequacy.
-16 to -1	A negative self-image.
0 to +16	An acceptable self-image.
+17 to +36	A positive self-image.
+37 to +48	A rather inflated self-image. Check your ego.

You've just completed an assessment of your attitude about yourself. It gave you valuable insight into your thoughts and feelings about yourself. The SI Inventory isn't intended to be used as a diagnostic test. Rather, it is a guide for self-analysis. It gives you a starting point for identifying areas of your attitude that may need adjusting.

Your Attitude About Others

Your attitude about yourself is important to the results you get in life. Similarly, your attitude about other people and external factors are crucial to your overall success in life as well. You have many areas in life—roles and responsibilities to yourself, to your job, to your family, and to your friends. In order to become effective in all these areas, you must begin by analyzing your thoughts about each area. Using the scale below, rate your perception of your attitude at home and at work: Your perception can be positive, negative, or neutral.

1. Circle the number that reflects your feelings at the moment.

2. Add the numbers that you have circled for the particular area.

3. Write your score on the appropriate line.

4. Interpret your score for each area.

Partial example:

At Home: **Negative**   **Neutral**   **Positive**
1. About your significant other   NA   -2   -1   0   +1   (+2)
Score:__4
(1.) _2_ + (2.) _1_ + (3.) _1_ + (4.) _1_ + (5.) _-1_ = 4

At Home:	Negative		Neutral		Positive	
1. About your significant other	NA	-2	-1	0	+1	+2
2. About your children	NA	-2	-1	0	+1	+2
3. About your mother	NA	-2	-1	0	+1	+2
4. About your father	NA	-2	-1	0	+1	+2
5. About your siblings	NA	-2	-1	0	+1	+2

Score: (1.) _____ + (2.) _____ + (3.) _____ + (4.) _____ + (5.) _____ = _____

At Work	Negative		Neutral		Positive	
1. About your boss	NA	-2	-1	0	+1	+2
2. About your co-workers	NA	-2	-1	0	+1	+2
3. About your agency/facility	NA	-2	-1	0	+1	+2
4. About the offenders	NA	-2	-1	0	+1	+2
5. About your job	NA	-2	-1	0	+1	+2

Score: (1.) _____ + (2.) _____ + (3.) _____ + (4.) _____ + (5.) _____ = _____

Interpretation

The score for each area—home or work—is the total of the point values given to its parts. A positive score indicates that you're exerting positive energies in that area of your life. Thus, you are probably enjoying positive results in that area. Congratulations! Keep up the positive attitude!

A negative score indicates that you are exerting negative energies and are probably suffering from negative results in that area. A score of zero indicates that you're exerting very little, if any, energy in that area and may be experiencing poor results—for lack of effort. In either case, you'll learn techniques for adjusting your attitude in the next chapter.

Chapter Summary

By completing the analysis of your attitude, you became more aware of your thoughts about yourself and the kind of energy you're exerting at work, at home, and in all areas of your life. Think of yourself as having a fully charged battery every day. In your battery is stored positive, negative, and neutral energy. Based on your attitude about yourself, another person, or a specific situation, you'll exert energy—in the form of action— toward your life at work and at home. Now that you have a better understanding of your attitude, what can you do to improve it? In the next chapter, you'll learn techniques for adjusting your attitude.

Leadership Series

Chapter Three

HOW TO ADJUST YOUR ATTITUDE

Chapter Objective

After completing this chapter, you should be able to:

• Use five attitude-adjustment techniques to improve the way you feel about yourself, change, other people, and responsibility.

You Are Only an Attitude Away

Do you believe that things simply happen to you . . . or do you believe that you have something to do with what happens to you? If you believe that life happens to you, the most you can do is have lots of luck, insurance, and disaster plans! You'll feel like a victim in the game of life, with little or no control.

> . . . if you believe that you can influence what happens to you, you'll feel like a "player" in the game of life.

However, if you believe that you can influence what happens to you, you'll feel like a "player" in the game of life. You'll understand that you're responsible for your own attitudes and actions. You'll learn to take responsibility for and gain control of your attitudes and, thus, your actions. You'll gain control of your life.

In this chapter, you'll learn several attitude-adjustment techniques for fine-tuning your thoughts about yourself and dealing with change and other people. These techniques can improve the quality of your life—at home and at work. Regardless of how satisfied you are with your life, this chapter holds opportunities for you to adjust your attitudes to become a happier, more positive person.

Attitude-Adjustment Technique No. 1: Listen to Your "Self-Talk"

You are communicating every waking moment of your life. At home, you communicate with your family. At work, you communicate with supervisors and co-workers. And when you're by yourself, you're still communicating . . . with yourself.

. . . experts say we spend 50 seconds out of every minute listening to ourselves instead of others!

In fact, even when you're in conversation with someone else, you're communicating with yourself. We call this self-talk. Self-talk is the inner voice that creates your thoughts, opinions, feelings, ideas, and, of course, your attitudes! In fact, experts say we spend 50 seconds out of every minute listening to ourselves instead of others!

You probably have heard the computer axiom, "Garbage in, garbage out." If you input bad data, you'll output bad data. Each of your attitudes is created in much the same way. If you fill your mind with bad thoughts, you'll experience negative attitudes. However, if you fill your mind with good thoughts, you'll enjoy positive attitudes, along with the good things that naturally follow.

We usually live up—or, in some cases, down—to our own expectations. We often become what we believe. For example, if you think, "I can't," then you won't! If you expect failure, you may not even try to succeed. If you expect success, though, you'll work hard to achieve it and chances are you'll do just that. To create positive attitudes, you must fill your mind with positive thoughts.

Eliminate your excuses and self-doubts. Replace them with positive thoughts, such as "I can, and I will become what I think." In sum, expect success!

Replace Negative Thoughts with Positive Thoughts

As we mentioned earlier, some negative attitudes come from comparing yourself with other people you believe are "better" than you. Your self-talk might sound like, "I can't do that because I don't have as much time . . . I'm not as good looking . . . I don't have as much money . . . I'm too old . . . I'm too young…," etc. These kinds of attitudes come from thoughts that you're not as good as other people.

Rechanneling your negative thoughts to more positive thoughts is a simple process. But don't expect success overnight. You need to keep practicing and practicing until the positive thoughts flow naturally—until they become a habit. The following chart shows you how to change your negative thoughts to positive ones. Pay careful attention not only to the words but also the feelings they evoke.

Negative Thoughts	Positive Thoughts
I'm a failure.	I've not yet succeeded.
I haven't accomplished anything.	I've learned something.
I made a big mistake.	I was confident enough to try.
I didn't get what I wanted.	I have to do something differently.
I'm inferior.	I'm not perfect.
I wasted my time.	I invested my time in future success.
I should give up and walk away.	I must work smarter.
I'll never do that again.	I'll be more patient.
That was a bad idea.	I'll look for a better idea.

In addition to redirecting your thoughts, also picture yourself being a success at what you want to be. If this sounds odd to you, remember that many successful people have overcome failure because they believed they could do so. They could see themselves being a success. For example, Abraham Lincoln failed twice in business, had a nervous breakdown after his sweetheart died, lost six congressional races, and lost the race to become vice president. Yet at age 52, he was elected president of the United States and is now remembered as one of the country's greatest leaders. Why was he so successful? He was confident, and pictured himself as being successful.

Attitude Adjustment

Think for a few moments about the areas of your life where you expect success. Write your responses in the spaces below.

At home, I can or will (I picture myself . . .):

_____

_____

_____

At work, I can or will (I picture myself . . .):

_____

_____

_____

Attitude-Adjustment Technique No. 2: Pursue Happiness

If you're feeling sad or depressed about a situation in your life, you may need to adjust your thoughts about it to become happy again. By definition, happiness is a state of satisfaction or contentment. Based largely on your expectations, you determine what makes you happy. Therefore, the higher or more unrealistic your expectations, the greater chance for you to experience unhappiness. You may need to reconsider your expectations in order to be satisfied or contented. Here are five ways you can find happiness in even the most unpleasant situations.

Option 1: Clearly Understand What You Want

The key to your happiness is understanding what's really most important to you—that is, knowing what you want most out of life. Your happiness may often get confused with your desires and things that you believe fulfill your desires. For instance, you might say, "I want a new red convertible." When asked to consider why you want it, you discover, "I want to have fun and excitement." The true desire is for fun and excitement; the convertible is simply a means to get fun and excitement.

How many times have you been disappointed or unhappy when something you desired didn't work out or happen the way you'd hoped? For example, suppose your bank came back to you and said you didn't qualify for a loan to buy the convertible. You might spend days or even weeks feeling sad or depressed about the situation. But the car is just one means of fulfilling your desire for fun and excitement. If you quickly recognize this, you'll be able to think of other ways to bring fun and excitement into your life. Perhaps you'll decide to take a vacation, join a club, or learn a new hobby.

In other words, if you know your true desires, you can create alternative ways to fulfill them. You can have fun without spending a million dollars or find love and happiness without being in a romantic relationship.

Option 2: Don't Wait for Happiness

Another obstacle to your happiness is waiting until something happens—or stops happening. If you're not content with the current situation, you may tend to believe that a person or a future event will bring you happiness. For instance, you might say, "I'll be much happier when I graduate...I move out on my own...I lose 25 pounds...I get a different job...I get married... my children move out of the house...or I retire."

Stop wishing your life away! You may not have a chance to enjoy tomorrow. Recognize the things at work, at home, and about yourself that are good. Life isn't perfect today, nor will it be tomorrow. Stop waiting for happiness to come to you—it may never find you. Instead, bring yourself happiness today by adjusting your attitude. Think, feel, and be happy! As Abraham Lincoln once said, "Most folks are as happy as they make up their minds to be."

Option 3: Tell Yourself, "This Too Shall Pass"

Another attitude-adjustment technique for making it through those "blue" days is to remember that pain won't last forever. The suffering or sadness you feel will disappear sooner or later, depending on the severity of the situation. To get through the healing process, tell yourself, "This too shall pass." You've survived other significant stressors in the past, and you will survive others now and in the future.

For instance, do you remember the pressure you faced as a teen—worrying about passing tests in school, completing school projects on time, and getting along with your friends, teachers, and parents? At the time, you probably thought that life couldn't get any worse! You survived not only those challenges but also probably many others as well.

Overcoming Events

Identify three stressful events that you have overcome in your life.

Age: _____

Event: _____

Age: _____

Event: _____

Age: _____

Event: _____

Option 4: Remember, Others Have It Worse

Self-pity is another form of unhappiness: Poor me . . . "I lost . . . or I don't have . . ." This kind of self-inflicted sadness often draws little, if any, sympathy from others. One way to overcome feelings of self-pity is to think about how fortunate you are. Think about other people who are less fortunate than you. As long as there is starvation, disease, and violence in our society, there will always be suffering. Think about walking in someone else's shoes, carrying their burdens, and struggling with their concerns. Remember, things could be a lot worse. Stop feeling sorry for yourself just because no one else will!

Gratitude List

List five things in your life that you are grateful for having.

1. _____

2. _____

3. _____

4. _____

5. _____

You can update and/or expand this list every few months.

Option 5: Deal with Depression

The most severe state of unhappiness is called depression. It is an emotional disorder marked by sadness, inactivity, and a difficulty in thinking and concentrating. It's the "down" time in your life. If you suffer from severe or long periods of depression, seek medical assistance. Do not try to self-medicate yourself with alcohol or drugs. Severe depression often requires qualified medical or psychological assistance. There is no shame in asking for help, and there is no need to suffer in silence.

The common signs of severe depression include:

Mood	Thoughts	Behavior & Appearance
Extreme sadness or doom-and-gloom attitude Excessive crying Loss of interest in activities, people, and appearance Significant and sudden mood variations	Pessimism concerning future Strong guilt feeling Low self-esteem Feeling of inability to go on Excessive self-blaming Difficulty in thinking, concentrating	Withdrawal or silence Loss or increase of appetite and/or weight Sleeping problems—too much or too little High anxiety or tension Downcast eyes/looks Lethargy (sluggishness, a stupor-like state) Writing or leaving suicide notes Talk of suicide Neglect of personal appearance

If you believe that your depression is mild and choose to deal with it yourself, rechannel your self-talk. What are you telling yourself about the situation? Why are you feeling sorry for yourself? Why are you feeling helpless? Why are you doubting your abilities? What are your opportunities?

The best cure for mild depression is to get up and get doing! Gain control of your emotions. If you can't deal with them by yourself, ask someone for help. Be sure that you trust the person and clarify the role you'd like him or her to play. Here are some ways that another person can help:

1. Listen to your thoughts and feelings.

2. Ask questions that can help you solve your problems.

3. Do some activity with you to help you get up and get doing.

Regardless of the role the other person plays, it's essential that any decision you make is your own. You need to feel that you've regained control of your life. Take one step at a time. Once you rechannel your energy in the right direction, results will follow.

Attitude Adjustment

Think about something in your life, at home, or at work that's making you sad, unhappy, or depressed. Then analyze the situation and try your best to find happiness by adjusting your attitude.

1. What do you feel sad, unhappy, or depressed about?

   _____

2. What did you expect from the situation?

   _____

3. What are your true desires in this situation?

   _____

4. Are you waiting for something to happen to change your feelings? If so, what?

   _____

5. Has something like this ever happened before? If so, how do you feel about it now?

   _____

6. Can you identify people who are in a worse situation than you are?

   _____

7. Who can help you resolve your problem?

   _____

8. How can you fulfill your true desires?

   _____

Attitude-Adjustment Technique No. 3: Seek Comfort with Change

Have you noticed lately that, wherever you go and whatever you do, the only thing you can count on for certain is change? It's all around you. There is absolutely no way to avoid change: It affects your family, your career, and your health.

Leadership Series

Why is change so difficult to accept? Why do people resist change? The diagram below illustrates your Circle of Comfort and how change influences it.

Your Circle of Comfort

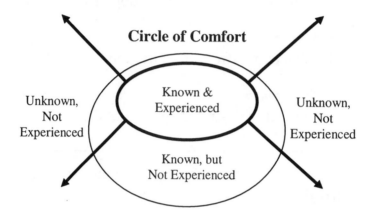

The area inside the innermost circle is called your Circle of Comfort. These are the activities and relationships in life with which you feel most comfortable or familiar. Your comfort comes from your knowledge of—and past experiences with—these activities and relationships. Examples of things you might find in your circle of comfort include activities from your past jobs and current job, neighborhoods you've lived in, and relationships with your family, friends, and co-workers.

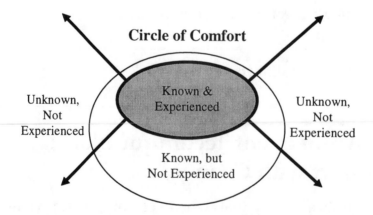

The size of your circle of comfort is a reflection of your exposure to the world. A small circle is a sign that you've limited yourself. A larger circle indicates that you've learned and experienced more in life.

American Correctional Association

The area immediately outside your circle of comfort consists of activities and relationships that you know about but with which you have no experience. You may approach this area with some degree of fear. Examples of activities and relationships in this area include seeking a different job in the same agency or joining a professional organization you've heard about from other members.

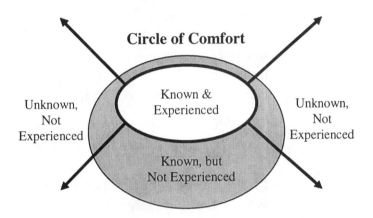

The outermost area includes all other activities and relationships—the ones with which you're least comfortable. You have little or no knowledge or experience with these activities and relationships. If you were exposed to one of them, you would feel the most resistance, fear, and apprehension. Some examples of activities and relationships in this area include moving to a new city or starting a new job or career.

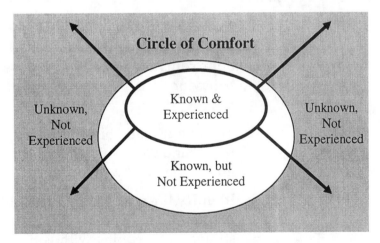

If you've recently experienced change and are feeling a bit unsettled by it, here are a couple of ways to find comfort.

Option 1: Face Up to Fear

Begin by recognizing that anytime you face an activity or relationship with which you have limited knowledge or experience, you will be afraid. It's a natural response. You learned about fear when you were a child. It sounded like this: "Don't do this . . ." and "Don't do that . . ." Fortunately, this fear probably saved your life on many occasions—when you looked both ways before crossing the street or passed up the opportunity to drink poison.

You used those early frightening experiences to learn what to do and what not to do. It's time once again to use your fear to learn and grow. Think about life as an adventure. Make waves. Don't be afraid to take risks. To risk nothing is to fail to experience life. To risk something is to think, feel, learn, and grow. If you never venture beyond the comfort of your own driveway, you'll miss out on what life has to offer.

Here are four tips for coping with fear:

1. **Expect a degree of discomfort at first; it's a natural part of change.** It will take approximately 30 days for any new behavior or habit to feel comfortable to you.

2. **Trust your fear.** Think of fear as your friend and companion in life. Let fear guide you, not hold you back.

3. **Identify the worst thing that could happen if you were to change.** Develop strategies for coping with your worst-case scenario so that you'll be prepared for the worst if it happens.

4. **Get started and take one step at a time.**
   Don't overwhelm yourself by trying to
   deal with the entire situation all at once.
   It's important to keep looking ahead and
   to let yourself become comfortable with
   each step of the change process.

Option 2: Expect Mistakes

Another aspect of change is dealing with the
results you get along the way and in the end.
It's often easy to give up on something when it
doesn't work out or happen just the way you
thought it would. Part of being successful means
recognizing that mistakes and failures are bound
to happen.

Adjusting your attitude to expect mistakes
will help you accept them as a natural part of
change and growth. If you aren't making mistakes, you aren't trying. It's impossible to succeed without making at least a few mistakes;
think of mistakes as the dues of success. For
example, Henry Ford forgot to put reverse gear
in his first car. Columbus was looking for a
quicker route to India when he found America.
Thomas Edison made 1,000 unsuccessful proto-
types before inventing the light bulb. He said,
"I didn't fail 1,000 times. The light bulb was an
invention with 1,001 steps."

Mistakes are valuable lessons: They tell you
to do something differently. Learn to expect mistakes. Use them as road signs on life's journey
to success. The biggest mistake you can make is
failing to try—you'll never experience success
if you don't try! And remember, "If at first you
don't succeed, try, try again."

Believe it or not, winners make more mistakes than losers. What do you remember most
about winners? You remember their victories,

not their failures. For instance, suppose a football team wins the Super Bowl. Do you remember this victory or the games the team lost during the season?

Attitude Adjustment

Think of a situation (an activity or a relationship) at home or at work that has recently changed and caused you discomfort. Analyze why you've been uncomfortable with the situation, and adjust your attitude to accept the change.

1. Identify an activity or relationship with which you're uncomfortable: _____

2. Identify the recent change._____

3. What do you know about the activity or relationship that might help you feel more comfortable?_____

4. What do you fear most?_____

5. What do you want from the situation? _____

6. Identify the first few steps you'll take to feel more comfortable with the situation:

   a. _____

   b. _____

   c. _____

Attitude-Adjustment Technique No. 4: Value Relationships

At home and at work, you deal with a variety of people who have a variety of backgrounds, experiences, opinions, and, of course, attitudes. It's virtually impossible to find another person who thinks, feels, and acts the same way you do. Therefore, your attitude toward someone else is largely affected by your willingness to accept and deal with his or her similarities to yourself—as well as the differences.

President Theodore "Teddy" Roosevelt said, "The most important single ingredient to the formula of success is knowing how to get along with people." One of life's greatest rewards, and one of its greatest challenges, comes from the relationships you develop in life. From the moment you're brought into this world until the time you leave, you need other people to survive. You'll find some of these people more enjoyable than others.

What constitutes a relationship? In its simplest form, a relationship occurs when two or more people share something. That something can be a park bench, a sidewalk, a highway, a hobby, an employer, or a house! A relationship may last for several moments or several years. Regardless of its length, your attitude toward the other person affects your behavior and influences the quality of the relationship.

Someone once said, "It's not the length of our life that matters most; it's the depth." In other words, it's not what you do that's important; it's how you do it. How healthy are the relationships you have with your co-workers and your supervisors? How healthy are the relationships you have at home—with your spouse, your children, and your parents? Let's explore several strategies for adjusting your attitudes toward others.

Option 1: Respect Other People

One of the best ways to let other people know that you value and respect them is to ask them for help. Yet, many times your attitude about asking for help prevents you from getting what you want. You may fail to ask for help because of your pride. You may fear that others will view your asking for help as a sign of weakness. If those thoughts have stopped you from seeking others' help, it's time to adjust your attitude!

Contrary to what you may be telling yourself, asking questions and requesting assistance:
- Indicates high self-worth and self-esteem.
- Lets others know what you want.
- Gives others the pleasure of helping you.
- Is better for your health, because it releases pressure and tension created by uncertainty.

Just as it makes you feel good when someone asks for *your* help, others will feel good if you ask for *their* help. Otherwise, by failing to ask family members, friends, and co-workers for help, you are being stubborn, selfish, and judgmental of others. Not giving someone a chance to help is depriving him or her an opportunity to grow.

Attitude Adjustment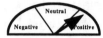

Identify a family member, friend, or co-worker with whom you're having a difficult relationship. List the skills, knowledge, and personality this person brings to your relationship.

Person: _____

Skills: _____

Knowledge: _____

Personality: _____

How can you tell or show that you respect or value this person's contribution to your relationship? (Example: "I appreciate your skills/knowledge/personality.")

Option 2: Forgive and Forget

Another way to adjust your attitude toward a relationship is to forgive and forget past actions. For instance, are you letting something that a friend did or said affect your relationship? Forgiving replaces negative thoughts with positive ones and prepares you to "give" again to the relationship. In fact, forgiving is one of the greatest gifts you can give a friend. And learning to forgive is one of the greatest gifts you can give yourself.

Attitude Adjustment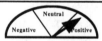

Identify someone who did or said something to you that has affected your relationship.

1. On a separate sheet of paper, write down the things that bother you most about the other person.

2. Identify at least five positive traits that he or she brings to your relationship. Don't stop until you have at least five!

    a. _____

    b. _____

    c. _____

    d. _____

    e. _____

3. In order to forgive and forget:

    a. Throw away the sheet of paper that has the bothersome traits about the person. Refuse to let those thoughts enter your mind ever again.

    b. Fill your mind with the positive traits you identified in Step 2.

    c. Erase the slate and start fresh to build a solid relationship.

Option 3: Communicate Your Expectations

Your attitude toward family members, friends, and co-workers is also affected by the degree to which they contribute to the success of your relationship. The challenge with any relationship—regardless of the number of people involved—is making sure that all the participants feel they are contributing and being treated equally. In the ideal relationship, each person contributes equally. For instance, in a marriage, each spouse assumes 50 percent of the responsibility for the success of the relationship. Inequity in a relationship creates resentment and bitterness —as you probably have noticed in the correctional environment where equality is impossible between correctional workers and offenders.

The key to achieving equity and, thus, success is open and honest communication. If you communicate your expectations, your chances of having a successful relationship are much greater. Another way to improve your relationships with other people is to follow the Golden Rule— that is, treat others as you'd like to be treated.

Your Golden Rules

Create your top ten rules or guidelines that you'd like others to follow when dealing with you.

When other people communicate with me, I want them to:

1. _____
2. _____
3. _____
4. _____
5. _____
6. _____
7. _____
8. _____
9. _____
10. _____

Now that you've created your Golden Rules, use them when you deal with other people. You'll probably find that what you give to others is what you get in return.

Option 4: Give and Accept Responsibility

As a parent or supervisor at work, one of the greatest compliments you can give to your child(ren) or staff members is a sense of responsibility. When you give someone the feeling of being responsible, you're saying:

- I trust you.
- I believe that you can do it.
- I want you to grow and develop.

Having responsibility means that someone trusts you and believes in you. The person wants you to grow and develop from the experience. He or she accepts you and your skills and, most importantly, your attitude.

Unfortunately, many of us resist responsibility. To adjust your attitude about accepting responsibility in a relationship, you must first clarify your thoughts and feelings about the responsibility. Do you think the responsibility is important? For instance, if you believe a task is busy-work and isn't important, you'll struggle against accepting the responsibility. However, if you believe the task is important, it's easier to accept the responsibility.

If you're not aware of the importance of the task, ask. Often, you may be given responsibility by someone who doesn't clarify it or communicate its importance. Take responsibility for your actions. If you don't know why you're supposed to do something, find out!

Service isn't a chore, it's an obligation. President John F. Kennedy said it best: ". . . ask not what your country can do for you; ask what you can do for your country."

Focus on ways you can contribute to or help the relationship, not on what you can get out of it. If everyone on a team, regardless of its size, focuses on adding value to the relationship, everyone ends up the better. Adjust your attitude toward what you can do for others.

Attitude Adjustment

Think of a responsibility at home or at work that you've been resisting. Analyze its importance and adjust your attitude toward it.

1. Describe your responsibility.

    _____

2. What is the desired outcome or result of having this responsibility?

    _____

3. To whom is the outcome or result important? Why?

    _____

4. What will you do to deal with this responsibility?

    _____

Attitude-Adjustment Technique No. 5: Stop "Shoulding" Yourself

There is one very damaging and paralyzing kind of self-talk. A voice within keeps telling you, "I should have . . ." or "I shouldn't have . . ." This kind of self-talk is called guilt. Guilt is frustration directed at yourself for something you did or did not do. Your guilt stems from your expectations of yourself. If you fail to live up to your own expectations, you become emotionally connected to the situation by feeling bitter, hurt, argumentative, cranky, testy, or aggravated.

A powerful attitude-adjustment technique is to stop "shoulding" yourself! Re-evaluate your personal expectations. If you believe something is important to you, do it; if it's not important, stop thinking about it and move on. But remember, you can never "should have done" anything. You either did it, or you didn't do it. After the fact, you have three choices. You can:

1. Continue to struggle or worry about it.

2. Pretend that you did or didn't do it.

3. Recognize that you did or didn't do it, and move on.

Remember, making mistakes is a part of life. They help you learn and grow.

If it's a missed opportunity, learn to find peace with yourself. What's over is over. Don't look back—that's not the direction you're headed. Look ahead and plan for the future. If the opportunity still exists, listen to your "shoulds" and do something about them. When you think or say, "I really should do something . . ." your conscience is talking. Your conscience can help you or harm you, depending on how you use it. If you ignore it and do nothing about your thoughts, they will haunt you until you feel guilty.

Transfer Your Should-Do List

Listening to your conscience can give you valuable information. Below are sample items on a Should-Do List transferred to a To-Do List.

Should-Do List	To-Do List
I really should start exercising.	Put a date and time on your calendar.
We should get together for lunch sometime.	Schedule the date and time right now.
I should do something to thank them.	Send flowers or a card to brighten their day.
I should stop biting my nails.	Ask a friend to hold you accountable.

Check Your Attitude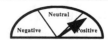

Let's evaluate your Should-Do List. For each item on your list, decide whether its important enough to do something about or whether you can just scratch it. Then create a To-Do List to help you accomplish the things that are important to you.

Should-Do List	Important?	To-Do List
1.	No Yes	1.
2.	No Yes	2.
3.	No Yes	3.
4.	No Yes	4.
5.	No Yes	5.

Chapter Summary

In this chapter, you explored five attitude-adjustment techniques for fine-tuning your attitude about yourself, your happiness, dealing with change, accepting other people, and coping with guilt. You learned techniques for replacing negative thoughts with positive thoughts and should-dos with to-dos. You discovered several ways to find happiness and overcome mild depression. You were challenged to face your fears and to expect mistakes during times of change and uncertainty. You gained an appreciation for respecting and forgiving others, following the Golden Rule, and accepting responsibility in a relationship.

In the next chapter, you'll identify ways to maintain a positive attitude.

Chapter Four

HOW TO MAINTAIN A POSITIVE ATTITUDE

Chapter Objective

After completing this chapter, you should be able to:

* Use five strategies for maintaining a positive attitude at work and at home.

Even when you have a positive attitude, you may have experiences at home or at work that drain your positive energy.

Preventative Maintenance

Even when you have a positive attitude, you may have experiences at home or at work that drain your positive energy. In this chapter, you'll discover strategies for maintaining a positive attitude in a negative environment and around negative people. Like physical exercise, this is mental exercise that you need to practice on a regular basis.

Attitude-Maintenance Strategy No. 1: Start Fresh Each Day

Regardless of what happened the day before or how much sleep you got, start each morning with a fresh outlook on life. As you get ready for the day, mentally prepare yourself by deciding what kind of attitude you'll have about the day's activities and the people you'll meet. Remember, you hold the remote control to your thoughts and feelings. The choice is yours, so make it a good one!

Give Yourself a Pep Talk

That's right. Just as coaches give their players a pep talk before a game, give yourself a pep talk before your day begins. Talk out loud or talk to yourself, but use your self-talk to fill your mind with positive thoughts and feelings. It's a good idea to use affirmations. An affirmation is a positive statement about yourself. By hearing your own affirmations, you'll create positive attitudes about yourself and the world around you. Examples of affirmations are:

> **Talk out loud or talk to yourself, but use your self-talk to fill your mind with positive thoughts and feelings.**

- I am positive.
- I am enthusiastic.
- I am motivated.
- I am happy.
- I am healthy.
- I trust my decisions.
- I follow through.
- I take action.
- I make things happen.
- I can do anything.
- I am lucky.
- I am successful.
- I enjoy life.
- I like myself.
- I am relaxed.
- I accept others.

Always express affirmations in the present tense and begin them with "I" or "I am." Write your affirmations on a piece of paper or on index cards. Put them where you'll see them often, such as on your bathroom mirror, in your daily planner, on your refrigerator, or in your car. Plant your feet firmly on the ground, stand straight with your chin up and look at yourself in the mirror. Take a deep breath, and read your affirmations aloud, boldly and confidently. You might even record them on tape and listen to them as you travel or do other daily chores.

Check Your Attitude

If you're feeling "blue" or you feel uncomfortable thinking positive thoughts about yourself, you may have difficulty writing affirmations. Remind yourself that everyone has positive traits. There are good things about you, and things that you do well. Think about your affirmations. Brainstorm positive thoughts about yourself but don't evaluate them. You may or may not firmly believe they're true today, but they're still statements of what you want to believe about yourself.

I am _____

I _____

I am _____

I _____

I am _____

I _____

I am _____

I _____

I am _____

I _____

Come back later and refine your list. Select the affirmations that are most important to you, and write them on a reminder card or piece of paper. This is the first step toward maintaining control of your attitude and your life.

Attitude-Maintenance Strategy No. 2: Clarify and Prioritize Your Life

Another way to maintain a positive attitude is to clarify what you want to accomplish in your lifetime. This strategy can help you understand your roles and goals in life. There are four simple yet powerful steps you can take:

Step 1: Clarify your purpose.

Step 2: Visualize your future.

Step 3: Set goals for yourself.

Step 4: Prioritize your actions.

Step 1: Clarify Your Purpose

We've all been given some responsibilities for adding value to life at home, at work, and in the community. We have a purpose. You must discover your purpose on your own.

A purpose is a simple, positive statement of why you are here. Like an affirmation, it also begins with "I am . . .," but a purpose is a specific description of a role you play in life. For example, "I am a happy and healthy person," or "I am a loving and caring husband or wife," or "I am an honest and trustworthy professional."

> **A purpose is a simple, positive statement of why you are here.**

A purpose isn't a goal statement. A goal is something you can achieve; a purpose is something you fulfill each moment that you're "in balance" with your life. Unfortunately, you may not clearly understand your responsibilities to others.

Discover Your Purpose

Give yourself plenty of time and freedom to discover your purpose. Some of the steps you can take are:

1. Identify and prioritize your most important roles in life, such as mother, father, professional, friend, and community leader.

2. List positive qualities that you aspire to, such as being caring, honest, and happy.

3. Narrow your list to a handful of one-
    or two-word phrases, such as patient
    and kind, hardworking, and happy
    and healthy.

4. For each major role in your life, write a
    purpose statement to describe yourself
    in that role, using all the appropriate
    phrases.

    For example:
    Role   Parent
    Quality   Loving and Caring
    Purpose   I am a loving and caring
                  parent.

5. Write a statement of your overall
    purpose.

Step 2: Visualize Your Future

... create a clear picture in your mind of what you want to accomplish in your lifetime.

You choose your purpose in life. Your next step, therefore, is to create a clear picture in your mind of what you want to accomplish in your lifetime. We all have hopes and dreams. The purpose of this step is to take those dreams and turn them into thoughts that are easy for you to understand—so you can become what you think about.

One of the most powerful techniques for achieving your life goals is through visualization. This is the process of creating a mental image of something you imagine happening in the future. The clearer your image, the stronger your belief and the more likely you'll take action to support that belief. You've heard the saying, "Seeing is believing." Well, if you can see it or visualize it in your mind, you will believe it. Believing in your dreams can motivate you to become what you think about.

An Example

A high school basketball team needed to improve its free-throw percentages. The team was divided into three test groups. The first group practiced shooting free throws for one hour every day for a month. The second group, the control group, did nothing. The third group visualized making free throws in their minds for one hour a day.

The first group that physically practiced shooting free throws improved their average by 2 percent. The second group, which did nothing, saw their average deteriorate by 2 percent. The group that mentally practiced making free throws improved by 3 1/2 percent!

This story demonstrates the power that visualizing success has on actual results. If you can imagine it and believe in it, it can happen— whether it's seeing yourself deliver a dynamic presentation to a roomful of people at work, moving into a beautiful home in the mountains, or dropping a 30-foot putt on the golf course!

Check Your Attitude

Think of something you'd like to do, enjoy, or accomplish in your personal or professional life. For instance, maybe you'd like to find the perfect job or career, buy your dream house, marry the perfect person, set an athletic record, or retire in an exotic location.

Close your eyes for a few moments and visualize what it might look like. See yourself doing it and enjoying it. Look at yourself. What are you wearing right now? Where are you? Are others around you? What are they doing?

On a separate sheet of paper, draw a picture of what you visualized. Use symbols and characters to represent your vision so you won't have to use words.

Etch this drawing in your brain. Post it in a spot that will remind you of your vision. If you can think it and see it, you can make it happen!

Step 3: Set Goals for Yourself

To help your dreams for the future become a reality, you need to set short- and long-term goals. A goal is something to aim for, something you want to achieve. It's a clear statement of actual behavior you want.

By defining your goals in life, it will be easier to stay headed in the right direction. Goals give you a reason to keep going; you need goals to survive.

For instance, in his book, *Man's Search for Meaning*, Victor Frankl writes about life in a concentration camp during World War II. He was one of the very few who survived the confinement. In the end, only 1 in 28 people survived. How did he survive while so many others perished? He observed that those who survived weren't necessarily the smartest, healthiest, most fit, or best fed. They were the ones who felt they had something significant left to do with their lives. For Frankl, it was his burning desire to see and touch his wife's face again.

> ... those who survived ... were the ones who felt they had something significant left to do with their lives.

It's critical to have both long-term and short-term goals. Short-term goals help you break up larger, long-term goals into more manageable steps. For instance, a long-term goal may be to retire at age 50 from your agency. Some short-term goals that may help you achieve that goal could be to:

1. Earn a bachelor's degree by age 25.

2. Establish an average salary of at least $30,000 by age 30.

3. Find ways to increase your annual income each year thereafter.

4. Contribute at least 10 percent of your annual income to a retirement account.

A valuable goal statement will meet the following criteria. According to management expert Ken Blanchard, it will be:

S   Specific. It is stated in descriptive terms, not in generalities. In other words, you can "see" the behavior.

M   Measurable. It includes dates and other quantifiable parameters to further define your goals.

A   Attainable or Achievable. You are capable of doing it.

R   Realistic. It is possible to do or achieve.

T   Timely. You have the time available to do it, and it is the appropriate time to do it.

For example, a valuable goal statement might be, "I will complete my graduate school program by next May with at least a 3.3 grade-point average."

After achieving a long-sought-after goal, you might feel a letdown until you clarify your next goal. For instance, have you ever gotten a cold after completing a big project? Have you ever stopped doing something completely after achieving a goal, such as reading a book or running a race? Your mind, heart, and body become so focused on a task that they become immune to other factors surrounding them. You exert a lot of positive energy into achieving a goal. So, when it's finally reached, you experience an energy slump, or letdown, until you jump-start yourself with another goal.

To provide steady fuel for your energy, create a list of long-term goals you'd like to accomplish in your lifetime. Break up each long-term goal into several short-term goals that will help you chart your progress toward the larger goal. Once you've achieved a goal, celebrate and reward yourself. Cross it off your list and move on to the next goal.

> To provide steady fuel for your energy, create a list of long-term goals you'd like to accomplish in your lifetime.

Check Your Attitude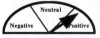

Identify and record some of your long- and short-term goals in life. Write at least one goal for each of the following areas in your life.

Family Goal

By _____ I will _____
　(insert date/year)

_____
　　　　　(describe the action you will take in specific, measurable terms)

in order to _____
　　　　　　　(insert results you hope to achieve)

Is this goal achievable?　❏　Yes　　❏　No

Is this goal challenging?　❏　Yes　　❏　No

Health Goal

By _____ I will _____
　(insert date/year)

_____
　　　　　(describe the action you will take in specific, measurable terms)

in order to _____
　　　　　　　(insert results you hope to achieve)

Is this goal achievable?　❏　Yes　　❏　No

Is this goal challenging?　❏　Yes　　❏　No

Career Goal

By _____ I will _____
　(insert date/year)

_____
　　　　　(describe the action you will take in specific, measurable terms)

in order to _____
　　　　　　　(insert results you hope to achieve)

Is this goal achievable?　❏　Yes　　❏　No

Is this goal challenging?　❏　Yes　　❏　No

Step 4: Prioritize Your Actions

The final step in gaining control of your life's plan is to prioritize your goals. With so many distractions in your life, it can be difficult to keep your priorities in perspective. You have responsibilities at home with your family; on the job with your boss, co-workers, and offenders; and in the community with your church, civic, and professional organizations.

You may feel like the juggler trying to balance several spinning plates on top of a row of sticks. Just as soon as you think you have all the plates (and areas of your life) in balance, you start to feel the strain and begin to wobble. Trying to do too much for too many people without taking time to refresh yourself can cause confusion, frustration, and physical and mental fatigue.

Don't complicate your life with things that aren't important to you. Think about how many plates you can juggle in life. Concentrate on the few that are most critical to your happiness and your purpose. Remove the rest.

Each morning, ask yourself, "What can I do today to help me reach my goal?" Simplifying your life will help you maintain a positive attitude.

Simplifying your life will help you maintain a positive attitude.

Attitude-Maintenance Strategy No. 3: Enjoy the Moment

Another way to maintain a positive attitude is to stop worrying about the past or dreading the future and just enjoy the present. Learn to appreciate the things that are going on around you right this moment. One way to enjoy the moment is to think about this saying: "The past is history, the future is a mystery. Today is a gift. That is why we call it the present."

Here are three options to help you enjoy the moment.

1. **Option One:**   Appreciate Life
2. **Option Two:**   Search for the Golden Nugget
3. **Option Three:**   Reward Yourself

Option One: Appreciate Life

People who are facing death have the greatest appreciation for the moment. A woman faced with terminal cancer told a class she was eager for Christmas. She was going to make it the best holiday she ever had with her family. Saddened by her situation, the entire class broke down into tears. The woman immediately came back strongly and said, "Weep not for me but for yourselves. I know this will be my last Christmas, so I will make the most of it. Don't wait until you know it's your last to make it the best. You may not have that chance."

Forget about the past and stop worrying about the future. You've got one chance at making the most of the moment; it will never pass your way again. Appreciate what you have in life and who you have to enjoy it with. Evaluate who and what is most important in your life. To help you with your evaluation, complete the following exercise.

Take a Moment . . .

Situation: You were just told that you have one month to live.

1. Who would you like to spend time with during your final month?_____

2. If money and health weren't issues, what would you like to do?

   _____

3. If you had a chance to live your life over again, what would you do differently? Why?_____

   _____

   _____

By completing the exercise, you identified the people in your life who are the most important to you. You also identified a goal that was important to your success. What have you been doing to achieve it? And finally, you identified an area in your life with which you may not be satisfied. If it's not too late to change, start now.

Option Two : Search for the "Golden Nugget"

Another way to enjoy the moment—especially when you are dealing with a difficult person or situation—is to search for the "Golden Nugget." Regardless of the person or the situation, there is usually something good about everything in life. In some cases, finding it may take time or looking beneath the surface. By recognizing the good, instead of dwelling on the bad, you'll be better able to accept and appreciate the experience.

Think, "A problem means an opportunity."

The first way to find a "Golden Nugget" is to think of problems as opportunities to do something differently. Don't let anything or anyone get you down. Rechannel your thoughts and comments to think more positively about a person or situation. Nothing is ever perfect. To expect perfection is to expect disappointment. Learn to emphasize the positive. As someone once said, "Give me a lemon, and I'll make lemonade." For example, one morning a traffic jam snarled traffic on a bridge for more than two hours. Most people sat in their cars expressing their frustration and anger over the situation. In fact, all but one young man reacted to the situation this way. He passed the time by lying on the hood of his car basking in the sunshine. He told a reporter that he was making the best of the situation—taking a lemon and making lemonade.

> . . . think of problems as opportunities to do something differently.

Take a Moment . . .

Lets try it out. For each of the described situations, identify the "Golden Nugget." In other words, think of an opportunity present in each situation.

Situation: You got a bad performance review. Your supervisor identified several areas that need improvement.

*Opportunity:*_____

Situation: You mislaid your keys somewhere in your home.

*Opportunity:*_____

Situation: The electricity in your house went out.

*Opportunity:*_____

Think, "Things could be worse."

Think, "Things could be worse."

The other way to find the "Golden Nugget" is to look for humor in a bad situation. Perhaps recognize that things could have been worse. For instance, here is an alternate way to think about each of the previous situations:

1. You could have been fired instead of just getting a bad performance review.

2. You could have had an 8:00 a.m. meeting that you'd have been late for because of car problems.

3. You could have mislaid the keys inside your facility instead of your own home.

4. You could have been left in complete

darkness when the electricity went out if you hadn't had candles and flashlights.

Option Three: Reward Yourself

A final technique you can use to enjoy the moment is to recognize and reward yourself. In any given day, you do so many positive things for yourself and others, such as reaching a goal, exercising, walking the dog, having lunch with a friend, completing a difficult task at work, or fixing dinner at home. You may have forgotten about these things or may not believe that they're of value because nobody said anything to you.

At the end of each day, recall what you did well and rejoice.

Don't rely on feedback from others to feel good about yourself. Find inexpensive ways to reward yourself. Perhaps it's taking a nice walk, calling a close friend, or playing with your child(ren) or pet(s). At the end of each day, recall what you did well and rejoice. Feel satisfied with your accomplishments. Remember, even the worst day holds something for you to take away—a lesson to be learned or an idea to do something differently.

To further help you get in touch with your attitude, keep a journal of your thoughts and feelings. This is a great way to express yourself. Chapter 6 includes an Attitude Action Planner to help you get started.

. . . keep a journal of your thoughts and feelings.

Attitude-Maintenance Strategy No. 4: Express, Don't Suppress, Your Feelings

One way to maintain a positive attitude is to openly express your feelings. Unfortunately, when you were growing up, adults often told you what to do with your feelings. For instance, you were told to "Stop pouting." "Stop crying." "Wipe that grin off your face." "Smile and be happy." "Quit giggling." As a result, you learned to suppress (keep them inside, to yourself) your feelings, whether they were happy or sad, serious or silly.

It isn't healthy for you or your personal relationships to withhold emotions.

Don't be afraid of what other people may think of you when you laugh or cry—except when you're dealing with offenders. Expressing your feelings is good for your mental health and for your relationships (with family members, friends, and co-workers) because it communicates your true thoughts about the situation. It isn't healthy for you or your personal relationships to withhold emotions. Communicating your feelings is just as important as communicating words. However, you must maintain control of your emotions when working with offenders. It is not appropriate to share your feelings with an offender.

Smile

. . . it's virtually impossible to think negative thoughts while you're smiling.

The most popular way to express a positive attitude is through a warm, sincere smile. When you smile, you communicate your happiness. It's a symbol of contentment and satisfaction.

So remember to take a long, slow, deep breath and smile. Feel good about yourself, the people around you, and your environment. The beauty of a smile is that it not only makes you feel good but also makes others feel good too. A smile is a sign of acceptance and appreciation. It says, "I'm glad to see you, and I respect you as a person." Therefore, if you extend a smile to someone, you're likely to get a smile in return.

Did you know that it's virtually impossible to think negative thoughts while you're smiling? Try it out. Think of someone or something that really made you mad. Create a picture in your mind. Now smile. Could you do it?

Laughter: A Healthy Mental Workout

Another great way to express a positive attitude and relieve pain is to laugh. You can laugh only when you're relaxed, and the more relaxed you are, the less pain you feel. When you laugh, endorphins are released in your brain that give you a "natural high"; your respiratory system gets a workout comparable to exercise.

> **When you laugh, endorphins are released in your brain that give you a "natural high". . .**

As you learned earlier, you had a great attitude as a child. You knew a lot more about having a good time than most adults. They tend to take life too seriously. If you make time to play, dance, sing, and laugh, you'll always be a kid at heart—and being a kid again is good for your heart. Discover what makes you laugh. Some examples include reading cartoons or comic books, watching funny movies, listening to comedians, or playing with children or pets. A mental workout of laughter is just as important as a physical workout of exercise.

Having a sense of humor can often break up a stressful situation. Being able to laugh at yourself or a relationship can help you accept or make the most of even the worst situations.

Cry

While it's very difficult for some correctional workers to consider crying, another way to express your feelings is through tears. Tears are a natural part of the healing process. In fact, crying is just as important for releasing your feelings when you're sad as laughing is when you're happy. Give yourself the opportunity and the time to heal from an emotional wound.

Check Your Attitude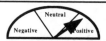

Identify three situations at home or at work where expressing your feelings is difficult. Describe how you can better communicate your feelings (with family members, friends, and co-workers) to maintain a healthy attitude.

Situation	Express
1. _____	_____
2. _____	_____
3. _____	_____

Attitude-Maintenance Strategy No. 5: Surround Yourself with Positive Influences

Your thoughts and feelings are most easily influenced through your senses . . .

The final strategy for maintaining a positive attitude is to surround yourself with positive influences. Your thoughts and feelings are most easily influenced through your senses— that is, from what you see, hear, smell, touch, and taste. Here are some tangible ways you can create a positive environment for yourself and others by appealing to your senses.

Appealing to Your Senses at Home and at Work

Positive Images

❑ Decorate your home with your favorite photographs of family and friends.

❏ Display plaques, certificates, and trophies of your accomplishments in your home (and, if appropriate, at work).

❏ Post your favorite poems, cartoons, and quotes in your home (and, if appropriate, at work).

Positive Sounds

❏ Listen to music at home or in your car that's appropriate to your desired feelings—upbeat music for energy or soothing music to relax.

❏ Sit outside and tune into the sounds of nature—the wind, the rain, the birds, or the waves.

❏ Find a quiet spot to meditate (e.g., focus on a positive thought or phrase and what it means to you) or just listen to yourself think.

Positive Smells (at home)

❏ Burn scented candles.

❏ Bake bread or pastries.

❏ Arrange or buy a bouquet of fresh flowers.

Positive Feelings

❏ Hug someone in your family or among your friends (outside of work).

❏ Exercise your body regularly—take a walk, jog, play golf or tennis, lift weights.

❏ Take a bubble bath or sit in a hot tub to relax.

Positive Tastes

❏ Eat regularly and maintain a balanced diet.

❏ Drink plenty of water each day to cleanse your system.

❏ Treat yourself to your favorite meal or dessert as a reward for doing something good.

❏ Savor your food, its different tastes and textures.

Check Your Attitude

Select several strategies for maintaining a healthy attitude through your senses. Refer to the previous list of ideas and add your own.

Positive Images

1. _____

2. _____

Positive Sounds

1. _____

2. _____

Positive Smells

1. _____

2. _____

Positive Feelings

1. _____

2. _____

Positive Tastes

1. _____

2. _____

Chapter Summary

This chapter presented five strategies to maintain a positive attitude. You learned how to start and end each day with positive thoughts. You explored the importance of setting goals for the future, while enjoying the moment. In addition, you were challenged to express your true feelings about life's ups and downs. With time and practice, these attitude-maintenance strategies will help you gain control of your attitude and your life.

Do you live with or work with someone who has an attitude problem? In the next chapter, you'll learn a process for dealing with the difficult attitudes of others.

> **With time and practice, these attitude-maintenance strategies will help you gain control of your attitude and your life.**

Chapter Five

HOW TO DEAL WITH THE DIFFICULT ATTITUDES OF OTHERS

Chapter Objectives

After completing this chapter, you should be able to:

- Describe why difficult attitudes can cause conflict.

- Identify the four choices you have in dealing with someone's difficult attitude.

- Use a five-step process for dealing with a difficult attitude.

It's much easier to maintain a positive attitude when you're surrounded by or you deal with people who have positive attitudes. Unfortunately, the correctional environment has many people with difficult attitudes. These individuals often exert negative energy that makes it hard for you to maintain your positive attitude. In this chapter, you'll explore strategies for rechanneling such negative energy in order to maintain and control your positive attitude.

Difficult Attitudes

. . . your goal in dealing with them is to maintain your attitude and not let them get you down.

Difficult people—you may encounter them at home, at work, in a store, on the telephone, or even while driving down the highway. You may think of them as "Defiant Dave," "Carol Complainer," "Roger Rough," "Nellie Never-Work," "Howard Who-Cares," or "Edward Ego"! Regardless of their attitudes, your goal in dealing with them is to maintain your attitude and not let them get you down.

Your Choices

People like to have choices. You like to choose the clothes you wear, the food you eat, the city you live in, and the job you have. From reading this workbook, you've learned that you also have your choice of attitudes.

When you deal with someone who has a different or difficult attitude, you have four choices—depending on how important the person and the outcome of his or her behavior are to you.

Option 1: Disregard the Person and Remove Yourself

If the other person isn't important to you, your first choice in dealing with the difficult attitude is to ignore it. For example, you may disregard a complete stranger's difficult attitude in a public setting because you have no relationship with him.

Option 2: Accept the Person and Remove Yourself

If your relationship with the other person is important, you may have more of an interest in his well-being. To maintain your relationship, you accept the person for who he is. You decide not to worry about or take action about his attitude or behavior. For instance, it may be the first time he has acted this way. Or, you may have other priorities that prevent you from investing time in dealing with the situation at this point.

Option 3: Accept the Person and Understand His or Her Attitude

Your third choice in dealing with someone's difficult attitude is to accept the person and try to understand his or her attitude. Until you understand how the other person thinks and feels about a situation, you may make incorrect judgments or false assumptions about him. To avoid these kinds of errors, invest your time in asking questions and listening with an open mind. This way, you'll gain a greater understanding of the reasons behind the attitude or behavior.

Option 4: Influence the Person's Attitude and Behavior

The final and, perhaps, most challenging way to deal with someone's difficult attitude is to try to influence the attitude and change the behavior. This option is the most difficult, however, because just as you have control over your attitude, other people have control over their attitudes too. You can only do or say things that can influence others' thoughts and feelings; others choose their own attitudes and actions.

. . . you may be able to change someone's behavior without affecting a change in the person's attitude.

Changing Attitudes

It is important to know that you may be able to change someone's behavior without affecting a change in the person's attitude. For example, an offender is told to clean up his cell Although he may do it because the correctional worker told him to, he still may think and feel that it's a frivolous task.

Changing behavior without changing the underlying attitude is a "bandage approach" to changing a habit. It's a short-term solution. The problem is most likely going to recur. To create a long-term solution, you must get the person to change his or her attitude as well as behavior.

Steps for Dealing with Someone's Difficult Attitude

The next several pages explain a five-step process for dealing with someone else's difficult attitude. The steps are:

Step 1: Determine your involvement.

Step 2: Understand the other person.

Step 3: Influence the other person's attitude.

Step 4: Resolve the problem.

Step 5: Recover.

> . . . consider how your attitude may influence the situation.

Examples of relationships that can benefit from using this process are those between or among:

- Parent and child

- Teacher and student

- Husband and wife

- Supervisor and staff member

- Correctional worker and offender

- Friends

- Relatives

- Peers

- Co-workers

Before using the five-step process, remember to consider how your attitude may influence the situation. It's always easy to believe that the other person has the attitude problem. Examine your own attitude and make appropriate adjustments before you confront the other person.

Step 1: Determine Your Involvement

Once you observe someone's difficult attitude, the first step is to determine what, if any, involvement you want with the situation. There are several critical questions you can ask yourself to help determine this. It's important to answer these questions on your own, perhaps in private, prior to confronting the person.

Question 1: *Is this person important to you?*

The first question identifies the importance of your relationship with the other person. Do you care about this person? Are you responsible for his or her behavior and well-being? For example, a parent cares for and is responsible for his or her child(ren). A supervisor is responsible for managing the behavior of his or her staff members.   A correctional worker is concerned about the behavior of the offenders under his or her care. In these situations, you would answer the question "Yes" and move on to the next question.

. . . determine what, if any, involvement you want with the situation.

Remove Yourself

If you answer "No" to any of the questions in Step 1, you should remove yourself from the situation or the relationship. Simply walk away or do not respond to the other person's attitude or behavior. This option is crucial to maintaining your positive attitude. For example, it's not a sign of weakness to walk away from an offender having a bad day but not posing any threat to you or others. Actually, it takes more strength to leave and ignore the taunts than to stay and become engaged in an unhealthy exchange.

Question 2: *Has This Happened Before?*

Everyone is entitled to an occasional bad-attitude day. Is this the first time you've ever observed this kind of attitude or behavior from the other person? If so, you may not want to worry about it. Answer the question "No" and remove yourself.

However, if you've observed this type of attitude before, you may want to deal with it to stop it from happening again—or from escalating to violent behavior. Bad habits or behaviors are best broken in the early stages of their development.

Question 3: *Does This Bother You?*

For every action, there is usually some type of reaction. Thus, if this behavior bothers you, it's best to deal with it instead of bottling up your thoughts and feelings. To avoid overreacting, you may want to give yourself some time to think about the situation before you answer this question. Often, a problem doesn't seem as severe the next day. However, if you have strong feelings about the situation, move on to the last question. But if you can tolerate the attitude or behavior, and it poses no danger to do so, remove yourself.

Question 4: *Are You Willing to Invest Your Time?*

The final question addresses two issues. First, are you willing to take the time to carefully and accurately communicate with the other person? Make sure that you'll have enough time to thoroughly deal with the problem. Second, is this a good time or place to acknowledge the attitude? If not, you may want to defer dealing with it for now and come back to it at a more appropriate or convenient time. For instance, it's not good to deal with an offender's difficult attitude when she's surrounded by other offenders who will take advantage of the situation.

> **Gather and write down all the facts about the behavior to make sure you can properly describe what happened.**

Prepare to Communicate

If you answered "Yes" to all the questions in Step 1, you determined that this person is important to you; this behavior has happened before; it bothers you; you have the time to confront the person about it; and it's a good time and place to have the conversation. Before you go on to Step 2, make sure that you're ready to communicate.

- Do you have all the facts about the behavior (dates, places, number of occurrences)?

- Are you in control of your emotions?

- Is this an appropriate time and place?

Gather and write down all the facts about the behavior to make sure that you can properly describe what happened. Also, write down questions you want to ask. Take this documentation with you.

Avoid discussing the situation when you and the other person are upset or angry. Calm down first. Also avoid embarrassing the other person by dealing with the problem in front of others, such as co-workers or offenders. Find a quiet location where you can discuss the situation in private.

Check Your Attitude

1. Think of someone with a difficult attitude who prompted you to simply get up and remove yourself from the situation.

_____

_____

_____

2. Why did you decide not to get involved?

_____

_____

_____

Step 2: Understand the Other Person

The goal of this step is to help you empathize with the other person. That doesn't mean you have to agree with him or her. You just need to understand the person's situation without passing judgment or making incorrect assumptions. You need to walk in her shoes to understand what she may be feeling.

> You . . . need to understand the person's situation without passing judgment or making incorrect assumptions.

Ask Questions and Listen to Empathize

The only way to better understand someone and validate your perceptions is to learn more about the situation. It's important to keep an open mind and a closed mouth during this step. Ask open-ended questions to learn the other person's thoughts and feelings about the situation. An open question requires more than a "Yes" or "No" response. In other words, ask who, what, where, when, why, and how questions to better understand what triggered the attitude and behavior.

Summarize the Person's Thoughts and Feelings

After the other person has shared her thoughts and feelings about the situation, communicate that you understand what she is thinking and feeling. You don't have to agree with the thoughts and feelings—just understand the situation. You can do this by restating the main points.

The model for this summary sounds like: "(Person's first name), I understand why you feel (summarize his or her feelings) and that you think (summarize his or her thoughts)."

Accept the Person

When you accept someone, you're not necessarily committing to liking or even respecting the person.

In Step 1, you determined that this person was important to you. Therefore, Step 2 seeks to maintain that relationship. When you accept someone, you're not necessarily committing to liking or even respecting the person. You're simply agreeing to accept the person for who she is, regardless of her opinions, personality, attitudes, and behaviors.

Do You Desire a Change in Attitude and Behavior?

The final part of Step 2 is to determine whether you'd like a change in the person's attitude and behavior. If you feel that a change in the person's attitude and behavior is no longer necessary, terminate the conversation by:

1. Expressing your appreciation for his or her feedback.

2. Offering future assistance or guidance.

However, if you still believe that a change is desirable, continue to Step 3.

Notice that determining whether you want a change doesn't occur until after you've discussed the other person's thoughts and feelings. Through your conversation, you may have clarified misunderstandings or incorrect assumptions. If you had not done so, you could make inappropriate comments or suggestions during the "influence" part of your discussion—Step 3.

> **Through your conversation, you may have clarified misunderstandings or incorrect assumptions.**

Check Your Attitude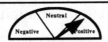

1. Think of someone with a difficult attitude with whom you recently spent time in an effort to understand his or her thoughts and feelings.

    _____

    _____

    _____

2. What did you learn from your discussion?

    _____

    _____

3. Did your conversation change your perceptions of the person's attitude? If so, how?_____

    _____

    _____

Step 3: Influence the Person's Attitude

The purpose of Step 3 is to help the other person recognize that his or her attitude is causing a problem. Unless the person agrees that a problem exists, it will be virtually impossible to create an attitude change.

Describe How You Feel

First, let the other person know how you feel about the situation. A quality relationship requires open and honest communication from both individuals. Because you spent Step 2 listening to the other person's thoughts and feelings, he or she should be more willing to listen to your feelings.

Begin by identifying the behavior that bothers you; then describe how it makes you feel. Be sure to focus on behavior, not the person. Instead of using "you statements" (for example: "You complain. . ." or "You've been late . . .") that put the person on the defensive, use "I" statements. The format of an "I" statement might be:

"*(Person's first name)*, **when you** *(describe the attitude or behavior you observed)*, **it makes me feel** *(describe your feelings)*, **because I think** *(describe your thoughts about the situation)*."

Check Your Attitude

Identify the most common difficult attitudes you encounter. Then describe how those attitudes make you feel.

Types of difficult attitudes *(for example: whiners and complainers)*

_____

_____

_____

That behavior makes me feel *(for example: I feel frustrated)*

_____

_____

_____

Explain Possible Consequences

You need to let the other person know what has happened or what might happen in the future if his attitude and behavior continue. Let him know what privileges may be lost if the behavior continues. Make sure that you're willing and able to enforce the consequences you impose. This is no time for idle warnings.

Suggest Other Ways to Think About It

Help the other person gain a broader perspective on the situation. Offer a more positive way to think about it and his or her contribution. Identify the benefits of handling the situation with more positive behavior. In addition, you may tell the person how his difficult behavior affects other people, such as co-workers, offenders, siblings, friends, and parents.

Invite a Reaction

Because you're trying to influence the other person's attitude, it's important to have him or her respond to your suggestions. Ask open-ended questions to elicit feelings about your suggestions. Then ask closed-ended questions to confirm his or her understanding that a problem exists. Examples of such questions are:

Open-ended questions:	*Closed-ended questions:*
"What do you think?"	"Would you agree?"
"How do you feel about that?"	"Do you know how to do it?"
"Why is that important to you?"	"Can you see my point of view?"

Gain Agreement That There's a Problem

The last part of Step 3 asks you to mutually agree that a problem exists. From your conversation, you might have discovered that the problem is the result of one of several things, such as:

- Lack of adequate training

- Inadequate communication

- Incorrect information

- Misunderstandings
- Unclear roles and responsibilities
- Unreasonable expectations

Be sensitive to the ownership of the problem.

Be sensitive to the ownership of the problem. Once again, avoid using "You" statements such as, "You need to... " or "Your problem is..." They tend to put the other person on the defensive instead of preparing him or her to deal with the problem.

Use sentences that begin with "We... " and "Our..." instead of "You..." to indicate your willingness to support and coach the other person. Share responsibility for fixing the problem. Once you receive agreement that a problem exists, move on to Step 4.

Step 4: Resolve the Problem

The purpose of this step is to determine possible solutions to the problem attitude or behavior by defining expectations for a similar situation in the future.

Define Future Expectations

To define your priorities, as well as the other person's, Step 4 asks you to determine what you're trying to accomplish. Your description, or goal statement, should summarize what's important to you and what's important to the other person. Through negotiation, you must arrive at a specific definition of the desired solution. In some cases, there may be no room for negotiation, such as when you're dealing with your agency's or facility's policies and procedures, laws, and other rules.

Mutually Discuss Solutions

Ask the other person to offer solutions for meeting the defined expectations in order to correct the problem or prevent it from happening again. The more ideas the other person contributes, the more likely it is he will accept responsibility for changing his difficult behavior. Offer your own solutions too. Don't evaluate or discredit any ideas until you've explored all possible solutions. Keep an open mind!

Agree on the Best Solution

After you've exhausted and evaluated all possible solutions, decide which one best meets the goal statement you established earlier. Whenever possible, ask the other person to select the best solution; that way, you'll get him to take ownership of the problem and agree to the change you desire.

If you're a supervisor, you may not have as many options to choose from due to the performance requirements of the job. You may have even fewer options when dealing with an offender, due to specified rules or procedures. So be specific about your expectations, and recognize your right and responsibility to disagree with, and even veto, the other person's recommendations.

Check Your Attitude

Future Expectations

Think of a current difficult attitude you're dealing with at home or at work.

1. Describe what you expect from the situation or the other person, and why.

    _____

    _____

2. List as many solutions as you can for meeting your expectations. Don't evaluate your ideas, just record them all.

    _____

    _____

Step 5: Recover

The final step in dealing with someone's difficult attitude is to recover from the experience and move on. This step occurs after the face-to-face discussion.

. . . recover from the experience and move on.

Regain Your Positive Attitude

At this point, you may feel frustrated, angry, disappointed, sad, or betrayed by the other person's difficult attitude. The first part of the recovery step is to bring your attitude back to the level of contentment or happiness you felt before.

Let go of your own negative feelings about the person. Separate the behavior from the person. In Step 1, you admitted that this person was important to you. Don't let this confrontation damage that relationship. Imagine yourself saying, "I like the person. It's his or her behavior that I dislike."

Follow Through with Your Commitments

Separate the behavior from the person.

Now you need to follow through with any commitments you made during the problem-solving portion of your conversation. If you agreed to help resolve the problem, do what you said you'd do. While you're at it, don't forget to monitor how the other person is doing on his commitments.

Recognize Changes in Attitude and Behavior

Encouragement is a large part of this final step. If you don't see an immediate change in the other person's attitude or behavior, practice patience. It takes time to change a habit. Give praise and encouragement for effort, not just accomplishment.

However, if you haven't seen a change over a reasonable time, confront the other person again about his difficult attitude or behavior. Begin with Step 1 to determine the extent of your involvement. After all, things may have changed. After several confrontations with the other person, where little or no change is made, simply terminate the relationship, if possible. In situations where you must continue the relationship—such as supervising a staff member or offender—continue to work on your own attitude. The choice is yours not to allow the other person's difficult attitude to ruin yours or to continually upset you.

Chapter Summary

In this chapter, you learned a powerful five-step process for dealing with other people who have difficult attitudes or attitudes that are simply different from yours. You discovered that you have a choice in dealing with other people's attitudes to preserve your own positive attitude. It's important that you don't let someone else's bad attitude influence your own good attitude.

Before using the five-step process, remember to consider how your attitude may influence the situation. It's always easy to believe that the other person has the attitude problem. Examine your own attitude and make appropriate adjustments before you confront the other person.

In Step 1, you ask yourself several questions to determine your involvement. You can remove yourself from the situation if the person is unimportant, if this is the first time you've observed the difficult behavior, or if the situation simply doesn't bother you. Conversely, if you're willing to invest the time to properly deal with the situation, Step 2 explains how to understand the other person by asking questions and listening to empathize with him. If you desire a change, the next step is to influence his attitude. Once you gain an agreement that there is a problem, Step 4 shows you how to resolve the problem. Step 5 explains how to recover and regain your positive attitude.

Next, you'll have the opportunity to practice the five-step process.

Practice with Your Own Case Study

As you learned earlier, attitudes are everywhere. Think of someone who has an especially difficult attitude. Now use the space below to record your strategy for dealing with his or her bad attitude using the five-step process you just learned.

Step 1: Determine Your Involvement

1. Is this person at all important to you? If so, why?

   _____

2. Has this happened before? When and how often?

   _____

3. Does it bother you? If so, why?

   _____

4. Are you willing to invest your time? If so, when and where will you discuss it?

   _____

Step 2: Understand the Other Person

1. Ask questions and listen to empathize. (Write out who, what, when, where, why, and how questions to ask the other person.)

   _____

   _____

2. Summarize his or her thoughts and feelings. (You won't be able to do this until you have had your discussion.)

   _____

3. Accept the person.

4. Do you desire a change in the person's attitude and behavior? (You won't be able to answer this question until you have had your discussion.)

   _____

Step 3: Influence the Other Person's Attitude

1. Describe how you feel.

    " _____, **when you** _____
      (Person's name)   (describe the attitude or behavior you observed)

    it makes me feel _____,
                              (describe your feelings)

    because I think _____."
                           (describe your thoughts about the situation)

2. Explain each of the potential consequences.

    _____

    _____

    _____

3. Suggest other ways to think about the situation.

    _____

    _____

    _____

4. Invite a reaction from the other person. (Record his or her reaction.)

    _____

    _____

    _____

5. Gain agreement that there is a problem. (Record his or her agreement.)

    _____

    _____

    _____

Step 4: Resolve the Problem

1. Define future expectations. (Record the things that you want, and the other person's expectations expressed during your discussion.)

    _____

    _____

2. Mutually discuss solutions. (Record some of your thoughts, but be sure to ask for the other person's ideas during the discussion.)

    _____

    _____

3. Agree on the best solution. (Record the mutual solution.)

    _____

    _____

Step 5: Recover

1. Regain your positive attitude. (Identify strategies for adjusting or maintaining your positive attitude.)

    _____

    _____

2. Follow through with the commitments you promised.

    _____

3. Recognize any change in the other person's attitude and behavior. Write down how you will give encouragement and praise (what you will say and do when the time and place is appropriate).

    _____

    _____

Chapter Six

HOW TO GAIN CONTROL OF YOUR ATTITUDE AND YOUR LIFE

Chapter Objectives

After completing this chapter, you should be able to:

- Assess your understanding of your attitude.

- Use the Attitude Action Planner to gain control of your attitude and your life.

This workbook has exposed you to the essential knowledge and tools for gaining control of your attitude and your life. This chapter will evaluate your confidence in using the knowledge and tools.

Self-Test

After reading this workbook and completing the interactive exercises, I can . . .

Topic	Level of Confidence				
Attitude Awareness	**Low**				**High**
1. Identify the major parts of an attitude.	1	2	3	4	5
2. Describe the three types of attitudes.	1	2	3	4	5
3. Explain why attitudes are so important.	1	2	3	4	5

If you don't know how to understand your own attitude, re-read Chapter 1.

Attitude Analysis	**Low**				**High**
4. Evaluate my self-image.	1	2	3	4	5
5. Rate my attitude at home and at work.	1	2	3	4	5

If you don't know how to analyze your own attitude, re-read Chapter 2.

Attitude Adjustment	**Low**				**High**
6. Explain how to gain control of my attitude and my life.	1	2	3	4	5
7. Describe at least five attitude-adjustment techniques.	1	2	3	4	5
8. Identify at least three ways to find happiness.	1	2	3	4	5
9. Explain at least three ways to improve my relationships with other people.	1	2	3	4	5

If you don't know how to adjust your attitude, re-read Chapter 3.

Topic	Level of Confidence				
Attitude Maintenance	**Low**				**High**
10. Describe at least five attitude-maintenance strategies.	1	2	3	4	5
11. List the four steps to prioritizing my life.	1	2	3	4	5
12. Explain three ways to enjoy the moment.	1	2	3	4	5
13. List at least five techniques for surrounding myself with positive influences.	1	2	3	4	5

If you don't know how to surround yourself with positive influences, re-read Chapter 4.

Attitudes of Others	**Low**				**High**
14. Identify the four choices I have in dealing with another person's bad attitude.	1	2	3	4	5
15. Explain the five-step process for dealing with another person's bad attitude or behavior.	1	2	3	4	5

If you don't know how to deal with other people's difficult attitudes, re-read Chapter 5.

Be Prepared

Before you attempt to gain control of your attitude and your life, you must be aware of several critical factors that will affect your success.

1. **You must have the desire to change your attitude and your bad habits.** Just think of all the benefits to you and others if you do change!

2. **Be patient with yourself.** Don't expect immediate results. Anytime you change a habit, your natural tendency is to resort to your old bad habits. Give yourself time to adjust.

3. **Changing requires a lot of dedication and work.** Take one step at a time. "If at first you don't succeed, try, try again."

4. **The process of change is continuous; it's never complete.** As soon as you stop changing, you stop growing. Make a commitment to lifelong learning.

5. **Eliminate all excuses for your bad attitudes.** It's time to take responsibility for your choices. Life is a choice, and it begins with your attitude.

6. **Hold firmly the remote control to your attitude.** Others will try to take it from you and control your thoughts.

7. **Find someone who can help you be accountable on a regular basis for your change in attitude.**

8. **Keep track of your progress.** Record your daily goals and results in a journal.

Daily Attitude Check

To increase your awareness and understanding of your attitude, begin recording your thoughts and feelings on a daily basis over the next 30 days. The Attitude Action Planner on the following pages may be reproduced for your daily records.

Just as you have a physical routine for getting ready each morning, take time to mentally prepare for the day. Review your purpose and affirmation statements. Choose the kind of attitude you want for your day at home, at work, or at play. Identify ways in which you can adjust or maintain your attitude during the day.

At the end of each day, take the time to feel good about yourself. Reflect and record your thoughts and feelings about the day. Identify what you accomplished and learned. Give thanks for what went well. To prepare your attitude for the next day, identify something you'll do again or do differently as a result of your day's experience.

Remember . . . the attitude you have is your choice, and you are just a choice away from gaining control of your attitude and your life.

Attitude Action Planner *

Today is _____

At the beginning of each day . . .

❑ Start with a fresh attitude.

❑ Give thanks for another day to experience and enjoy.

✔ I feel _____ because I think

_____

✔ My attitude for today:

I will be _____ because _____

_____

✔ I will demonstrate my attitude today by: (*Describe your specific actions.*)

1. _____
2. _____
3. _____

✔ Through my attitude and actions today, I hope to enjoy these benefits and/or results:

1. _____
2. _____
3. _____

* *Note: Before you use this form, make several copies of it for your daily use.*

At the end of each day . . .

❑ Reward yourself.

✔ Today, I adjusted my attitude by: _____

_____

_____

✔ Today, I maintained my attitude by: _____

_____

_____

✔ Today, I dealt with someone else's difficult attitude by:

_____

_____

✔ Overall, I would evaluate my attitude today as: (check one)

    ❑ Negative

    ❑ Neutral

    ❑ Positive

✔ Based on today's experience, I will maintain or adjust my attitude tomorrow by: _____

_____

_____

_____

A Word from the Authors and Publishers

Attitudes are everywhere and everything in life! You simply can't go through a single day without them. Your attitude today creates your actions, which produce your results. By gaining control of your attitude, you will gain control of your life.

Our hope is that this workbook has touched your life and that you have been inspired to do something differently as a result of experiencing this workbook. We would like to hear how this workbook has helped you gain control of your attitude and your life. Drop us a short note by mail or fax to:

The American Correctional Association
Professional Development Department
ATTN: Educational and Training Products Manager
4380 Forbes Boulevard
Lanham, MD 20706-4322
FAX 301-918-1900